Listening to Your Body to Really Live Your Life

by

Donna Marie Vigilante

Mountain Yoga & Healing, LLC Press Books are
available for order through Ingram Press Catalogues

Mountain Yoga & Healing, LLC
Visit my website at http://reallylivingyourlife.com/
Email me at yogii500@msn.com

Printed in the United States of America

First Printing: 2014
by
Sojourn Publishing, LLC

ISBN: 978-1-62747-066-7 Paperback
ISBN: 978-1-62747-068-1 Hardback
E-book ISBN: 978-1-62747-067-4
LCN Pending

Dedication

to
James and Troy
I am alive and thriving
because of my love for you

Testimonials

After 8 months of surgeries, chemo, and radiation, my body was left with chronic aches/pains, fatigue, and weakness I had never experienced before. I knew that I needed someone to teach me how to not only rejuvenate my body, but also my mind and spirit. I am glad to say that yoga with Donna Marie has done just that. Now, 2 years later, I have gained back my strength, flexibility, and stamina, but most importantly I have learned how to listen to my body and how to live in each moment. M.W.

I've suffered with chronic upper back pain for over ten years. My right shoulder was visually 1-2 inches lower than my left when I begin yoga classes with Donna Marie. I'd been to many doctors and physical therapists with no luck and decided to face the fact that I would be in pain for the rest of my life. Since practicing yoga the pain on the left side of my back is practically gone and my shoulders are even with each other. B.S.

For years my doctor suggested that I try yoga to help with pain from Fibromyalgia, chronic fatigue syndrome, and an autoimmune disorder. I took ever-increasing numbers of medicines and had several body parts removed in the quest for that "magic" cure. I sat at home day after day, resting from no exertion whatsoever, feeling more and more despondent. It took all of my energy to drive my kids where they needed to go and to keep up with the laundry. Yoga didn't help me. Donna Marie Vigilante helped me help myself. J.P.

I've learned from Donna Marie that emotional well-being can be achieved through other means besides just meditation. J.C.

Contents

Acknowledgements

Special thanks to a number of women who have supported and helped me over the last several years: Karen Perleoni, Missy Garland, Joyce DeVooght and Christine Jalbert. Thank you for your love, conversation and friendships.

Michelle Bornmiller, my cousin and soul sister – thank you for your love, sharing my life, long conversations, our healing journey and your home whenever I've needed to get away.

A sincere thanks goes to Jackie Palmer, Missy Garland and Gene Culver for being another pair of eyes editing this book.

Thank you to my long time best friend Cindy Porter for her love, loyalty and artistic point of view.

Thank you Rj Piazza for your photographic abilities. You always bring out the beauty in me.

I want to also thank Rama Jon at Sojourn Publishing for your patience, kindness and words of inspiration.

Special thanks to William James Wehnes, one of my greatest supporters. William has truly shown his support over the years by providing assistance, love, and a true belief in my abilities. William has given much of himself in true friendship and without his sincere support and dedication I would not have reaped the success of my hard work.

I am sincerely grateful to Clifford Arnold, my long time friend and editor, for his deep belief in my intelligence and capabilities even when I doubted myself.

To every student who walked through the door at Mountain Yoga & Healing, whether you came once or have been with me throughout my nine-year journey, thank you for making me the teacher and vessel for healing that I am today.

Most of all, my grandmother, Margaret (Peggy) Travisano, my love – I miss you.

A Note to the Reader

This is not your ordinary book of healing. This book is about my experience on the journey to healing my physically, emotionally, and psychologically devastated life. As a result of those experiences, the biographical chapters are difficult for me to express because they are difficult for me to relive. The writing style is conversational and is written in my voice. I do not profess to be a professional writer. Therefore, I count on the reader's indulgence and hope they will understand the difficulty of writing about my traumatic childhood.

Throughout the book I have purposely altered the word disease to reflect the true energy behind the word for my work. The word will be presented as *dis-ease*.

The first rows of pictures of me on the front cover are 19, 23, and 24. While the picture on the bottom row was taken when I was 47.

Introduction

"It is estimated that 90 percent of all physical problems have psychological roots. That may sound like a gross exaggeration. In fact, it's probably a conservative estimate. A growing body of evidence indicates that virtually every ill that can befall the body–from acne to arthritis, headaches to heart disease, cold sores to cancer is influenced, for better or worse, by our emotions."

— *Pg. 3 Feelings Buried Alive Never Die...*

I n an age of stress related diseases and spiraling medical costs, there is an ongoing debate on health care. We spend billions each year and yet an embarrassingly high number of people live daily with chronic pain and/or *dis-eases* that will slowly kill them or leave them living with debilitating pain. Our health care system is allopathic in nature; it treats the symptoms and not the root cause of our pain and *dis-ease.* Many if not all stress related *dis-eases* have a root cause. When the root cause is not addressed, a person cannot fully heal their physical pain and suffering. I have learned from traveling through my own healing journey and guiding my youngest son Troy on his healing journey, that healing begins with choosing to honor your body's inner knowledge and trusting your feelings. My journey helped me to remember that this knowledge is always within. All people have the ability to heal themselves when they are able to reconnect with their own internal navigational system. The information I am presenting in this book is an invitation for you, the reader, to go on your own journey in order to transform one person at a time from pain to health, and in turn, to help transform the world.

In our society we have come to depend on doctors far too much for healing stress related *dis-eases*, which I believe are created by our choices and lifestyle. High *dis-ease* rates are a national public health problem primarily because people aren't taught that they can heal themselves. It is not that physicians cannot help us on this journey because there are many who are trained in a more holistic approach. However, to heal the body, the focus should not be primarily on relieving symptoms with the use of prescription drugs, invasive tests and surgery. It should focus instead on the person and the root cause(s) of their *dis-ease*. A more holistic approach involves investigating not only a person's physical body and their symptoms, but the emotional, mental, spiritual and social conditions as well. Our health system needs to keep us healthy using this approach versus the system we have now, in which the incentive is mostly a financial and a quick fix for the person in pain. Lots of institutions profit from illness and pain: the pharmaceutical companies, insurance and medical supply companies to name only a few. Anyone can learn how to listen to his or her body, regain their health and reduce their long-term dependency on the medical system. With health comes happiness.

I am living proof this can happen. I found my way back to physical and emotional well-being. It is an internal journey that you can learn to traverse on your own, for the most part; along with guides like me who can help you on your journey. Many people helped me to go inward and there I have found that everything I needed to heal myself was actually given to me at birth.

I finally figured out after years of suffering with physical pain that I was going in the wrong direction. I needed to make different choices and go in another direction. Going in the wrong direction means you've made a choice that goes against your inner knowing or highest good. Physical pain is your body's way of communicating that your emotional, psychological, and spiritual bodies are out of balance and need your attention. Let's look at an example, using your physical body, to describe going in the wrong direction. Many people slouch when they are working at their desk and their lower back bulges out; however, the correct direction for your spine is to be long and erect. The pain in the lower back is the body's way of communicating with you that you are going in the "wrong direction."

Another example of going in the wrong direction in our everyday lives is our inability to listen to ourselves. I was a divorced mother with two sons, working as a waitress on the weekends and attending junior college part-time. I was also in psychotherapy working through horrific childhood abuse and my impending divorce. My schedule at home was full like any other mother. My plate was full and yet I was unable to say no to family members and friends who asked me to do things for them. My inner being was screaming NO and yet out of my mouth came a yes. I was divided within myself because I didn't want anyone to be mad with me and yet I didn't have the time or energy to help him or her. I would have pain in my stomach, get a headache, or have an anxiety attack if I tried to tell them "No, I am too busy." In yoga when you feel pain, you know something's wrong and you're taught to back out of a pose and go in another direction. This is often hard because most of us have been raised that backing out is a sign of weakness. We won't consider backing out of any of our obligations, which is why we generally will not choose to go in an alternative direction until we're suffering and in constant pain. This pain solidifies in our bodies and is unable to be healed by medical efforts.

Many people I work with as a yoga instructor and energetic healer have suffered with chronic pain for years and most have had surgery and are taking a plethora of prescription drugs, both of which alter the body. So remembering and reconnecting with their internal navigational system is not usually what most people want to hear as the answer to getting out of pain. Most people want to get out of pain today. The thought of committing to the process of finding the root cause of their pain takes more time. It is an inward journey that must be taken alone and can seem foolish. While many of us did not cause the problems we face (sexual, physical and psychological abuse), we don't want to admit that we are 100% responsible for our own choices as adults and that all of our choices have consequences.

Like many people, I spent much of my life looking outward for happiness without realizing that the real answers lay within. Healing is within you, exactly like love. I work with many people who search throughout the world to receive validation that they are lovable. I often tell my students who are looking for answers outside themselves that we are like fish swimming around in water looking for the water. The answers lay right inside of you. Your internal navigational system can help lead you back to health and happiness.

Using this very process ultimately cleared every physical ailment and mental disorder that I was told would plague me the rest of my life. My life from the earliest time went from one disaster to another. As a matter of fact, I was often called "walking chaos". Similar to the 'Pigpen' character in Peanuts, all the dirt that followed me was chaos and pain. The gravity of all this extra baggage dragged me down. Yet through this journey, I found a way to create a heaven out of hell.

The objective of this book is to empower the reader, using my life as a testament, to the power of healing one's own life. I want to inspire you to begin to navigate through your feelings and body and allow them to take you on a journey out of pain. Learn how to use your own inner navigational system naturally given to you at your birth. As the good witch Glinda, said *In The Wizard of Oz*, "You've always had it in you."

I cannot imagine what my life would be like today at fifty, or if I would even be alive, had I not discovered the ability to listen to my body and feelings when I was in my mid-twenties. Back then I was consumed with physical, emotional and psychological pain. I was filled with anger, rage, resentment, bitterness, guilt and shame. I finally hit the wall because it was too much. It was only then that I began a slow, often-unfocused, journey inward while relearning to trust my own body and feelings as I did before I was abused. That journey led me to what I now call my 'internal navigational system' that I used to guide myself back to complete health and well-being. I slowly healed myself of every *dis-ease* and psychological disorder that once had overwhelmed me.

I use my internal navigational system to guide me daily, and I now teach this method to my students, family and friends. That's not to say I'm not faced with everyday life events that need to be addressed. However, today I now have the confidence that my body and feelings will guide me to my highest good, and I have no chronic pain or *dis-ease*. I am humbled to share what I have learned from my journey with you.

For the last 25 years I have traveled along a healing journey and from that journey this book was born. That journey taught me that I could not only heal my life, I could thrive and have anything and everything I could imagine. And so can you.

I will never be the person I may have been before the abuse, and yet I am a whole person created from the pieces that were left. My cousin Michelle, an acupuncture physician answered me this way when I asked a question about my constitution (your original energy when you are born). "Donna Marie, like Humpty Dumpty you fell off the wall (I believe I was pushed) and all of your pieces were shattered and we put the pieces back together as best we could."

Today, all you can see is a vibrant healthy woman who is on an extraordinary voyage in life. I have lost all of my excess weight and my face has cleared up and is beautiful after years of adult-onset acne. I no longer have fatigue, allergies, arthritis, cancer, or shingle attacks. I have cleared every chronic pain in my body. I am healed physically and emotionally and also have healed all mental disorders and am free of the disabling effects of those disorders, including the PTSD.

This book is based on that voyage and the information I gained that ultimately healed my life. I was told so many times by doctors and psychologists that I needed to accept that I had survived, and they would help keep my rage and *dis-eases* at bay by the use of prescription drugs and invasive procedures. Yet, I wanted to thrive and be pain free and healthy.

I look younger and brighter now at 51 than I did at 19 and I am thriving. I have both a Master's in Psychology from the University of North Florida and a law degree from Stetson University College of Law. I opened my own yoga studio eight years ago and business is going extremely well. Currently, I help others heal their minds, bodies and spirits from chronic pain, trauma, and every day stress. You don't necessarily need to have gone through all I did to be in chronic pain or just plain depressed and unexcited about life. The beauty of sharing my life and this information is this: If I was able to heal my life, then anyone and I mean anyone can heal his or her life. I am a living testament to the healing power of listening to your body and feelings to help navigate yourself back to health and happiness.

Chapter 1
Background – A Little of My Story

"The Mad Hatter: Have I gone Mad?
Alice: I'm afraid so. You're entirely bonkers. But I'll
tell you a secret. All the best people are."

— *Alice in Wonderland*

I would like to start with the fact that this is my version of what I experienced growing up in my home. As with all stories there is my truth, my family's truth and then the whole truth. My mother was pregnant with me and married at fifteen years old. She then gave birth to both of my brothers before she was twenty. At some point my mother crawled into a bottle to escape a reality she did not or could not face. The verbal and physical abuse she dealt out to my brothers and I was intense and terrifying. I walked on eggshells my entire childhood and long into adulthood. I cannot speak for my brothers; however, I know they both suffered immensely. Both my brothers and I ended up in jail with one brother spending at least 15 years in prison.

I was sexually abused as a child from the ages of two through thirteen, then violently raped in a steel crushing plant at sixteen, and almost murdered by this same man at twenty-one. My father, his father and one of my father's brothers committed all the sexual abuse. There are others to this day who suffered at the hands of these men and have not come forward. Being raped in a steel crushing plant at the age of sixteen sealed my emotional, psychological and spiritual destruction for a very long time. This led to years of being revictimized sexually because I felt unable to protect myself.

However, this was truly just the start of my downward spiral because at age sixteen I began to do serious damage to myself beginning with abusing drugs. At first, it was just fun, but then I realized I could kill the pain and block out my feelings. I became sexually active early, always requiring attention. I was raised to be a good Catholic girl and as they say, "I was 'til I wasn't." At the time, being raised Roman Catholic meant not questioning authority, just blindly following on faith.

The church I attended taught that a person 'sinned' when they had sex outside of marriage for any reason. When I asked Sister Mary Ann where in the Bible that was written, she got upset and believed me to be a troublemaker who was already having sex with boys. She said, "You will have to take it on faith," and then she asked, "Why are you asking such a question?" I wanted to read the Bible for myself to understand why my abuse meant I was going to hell because certain men in my family were molesting and raping me. Yet, I was terrified to tell her the truth and knew not to open my mouth. After class she called my mother and told her that I was nothing but trouble and was surely on a path towards hell if they didn't do something with me. I walked away from the Church and all its precepts after that.

I decided right then and there that if I was already going to hell, I was going there on my terms. That was the beginning of one of the darkest chapters of my life's journey. For the next 14 years I nearly destroyed my life – and to complicate matters, I was pregnant with my first son, James.

James was conceived the night his uncle and namesake was killed in a moped accident coming home from a bar. I was seventeen. My ex-boyfriend, Timmy, James' brother, was also seventeen and he had to identify the body and call James' parents who were on vacation and notify them of his death. Timmy called our house around 3:00 a.m. and came over. I was his ex-girlfriend and knew I had a kind heart he and would be safe with me. James was conceived that morning. I didn't marry Timmy. Just before Timmy's 43rd birthday, James found his father dead from alcohol poisoning.

I was 18 years old and had lived with Timmy for less than a year when I moved out of the trailer we attempted to share. My mother came to pick me up at 5:00 a.m. because I called her to tell her Timmy was passed out drunk, and I had a butcher knife in my hand and if he woke up and came after me one more time I was going to kill him. A few weeks earlier he received eight stitches in his leg after we fought. I was unable to contain the rage and anger I swallowed during years of abuse as a child, and I used it to protect myself. However, I was unbalanced and very dangerous.

At nineteen and living with my mother, I worked during the day as a waitress and was up freebasing cocaine in the evenings after James went to bed. When James was almost two, I stayed up for three days straight with little sleep and without eating or drinking water. On the third day, coming home from work with James in the car, my body gave out and I fell asleep at the wheel of my car and we had a head-on car crash with a 70 miles per hour impact. It's a wonder we survived. I knocked my front teeth out, broke my jaw and had 19 stitches in my lower lip. My knee was also operated on. This is when I truly began to abuse cocaine to numb the pain. The only good thing about all of this was that James didn't have a scratch on him.

I unconsciously almost killed myself because I was up for three days doing freebase cocaine, which my father had turned me onto. I waited tables and sold pot and cocaine to offset the cost of my drug habit and to help my mother pay the bills, which didn't last long. As mentioned earlier my mother had had three children before she was 20, didn't graduate high school but received her GED in her late 20's to persuade me to finish high school. She was a stay at home mom without any marketable skills when my parents divorced, and she was earning minimum wage.

My parents were divorced after years of my father cheating and making his decision to move his girlfriend from New Jersey to Florida. My father eventually married her. I also learned when I was 40 that I have a half-brother from another affair my father had during his marriage to my mother. My relationship with my father and most of his family is irrevocably damaged.

Looking for a fresh start and not wanting to face the truth about my life, I moved back to New Jersey after getting engaged to my father's sister's boyfriend. I first met Billy while they were dating. He was older and seemed mature and stable. He was a fireman and a high school track coach. Billy usually took James to the babysitter first thing in the morning since I generally worked the late shift at Houlihan's and didn't get off work till at least 3:00 am.

On this particular day I was off from work and James was at home with me. He was about two years old. For whatever reason, I had this gut feeling to look out the window. I saw my uncle who raped me in the steel crushing plant at sixteen pull down the street and park his car. Days before he had shown up at Billy's home. My grandmother (my father's mother) had told him I was now living in the neighborhood. Somehow in his warped mind my uncle tried to convince me he was in love with me and wanted me to have sex with him again. I was terrified because I knew what he was capable of. I was also naïve because I had told him I would tell Billy that he raped me if he came anywhere near me. Now, at twenty-one I was watching him walk to the trunk which was in the front of his old VW and take out a pair of gloves and a crowbar. I knew at that very moment he'd come to bludgeon me to death.

I only had a moment to find a place to hide. The landlords were out running errands and I was in the downstairs apartment alone with James. I checked all the locks on the door and made sure the windows were locked and the blinds were lifted so he could see into the apartment. I had to do this in a matter of seconds. I scooped James up and ran to the bathroom closet.

I left the closet door slightly open and hid. The way the apartment was set up you could walk around the complete house and see everything. I heard him rattle the outside door and move to the windows. He walked around the apartment rattling every window as he checked them. I stayed in that bathroom closet with every muscle shaking and James crying. I whispered in his ear, 'It will be all right'. I stayed in the closet for another half hour before I found the courage to crawl out on my hands and knees to make sure he had left. I left James sitting in the bathroom closet.

Once I knew he was gone, I called Billy at work. However, instead of telling him what had happened, I said that I hated the cold, missed my family and couldn't live there anymore. I wanted to go home immediately! I left Billy and went back to Florida. A few years later my uncle's son shot him in the head and killed him.

Billy was deeply in love with James and I and had asked me to marry him. My life was better than it had ever been; however, instead of telling him the truth, I automatically fell into a pattern, developed from years of abuse, when I was taught NEVER to open my mouth. At this point, I was 21 years old. I felt so guilty and shameful that I wasn't able to talk with Billy and tell him the truth. So, I did what I did best at the time – RUN. Run from one painful experience to another.

A few years after this, still running at warp speed from anything resembling addressing my pain, I got pregnant with my second son, Troy. This is when I married Dennis, Troy's father. I got married because my mother said, "Who the hell do you think you are, having two children and not getting married?" So I married a full-fledged angry alcoholic, just like my mother, except he was 6'5" and I was 5'2".

He loved Crown Royal and pain pills. He abused me emotionally and verbally came after me when he drank and because I was filled with so much anger, I went right back at him. When he wasn't drinking, Dennis and I got along really well. However, both of us were in a lot of emotional and psychological pain and we took it out on each other.

I was now 24 years old, and my face exploded with acne. My allergies created havoc in my life because I couldn't breathe most of the time. It is amazing how much marijuana I was smoking at this time. I would start in the morning (called 'wake and bake') and smoke until till I passed out at night. When I couldn't sleep I would just get up and smoke some more.

I began therapy at this time because my life was out of control, and my two sons were caught up in the middle of my insanity. My life had so much chaos and drama I cannot put it into words. I also went back to school part-time.

When I left Dennis, I was not starting all over. To start over you start at zero. I, on the other hand, was a lot further down than zero. I had a hard road ahead of me. I was now a single mother of two sons under the age of nine and waiting on tables for a living. I was in remedial classes at the Junior College and flat broke. And my family was not in a position to help me.

After finally divorcing Dennis, several years later I married Nelson, who was five years younger than I was. By this time I had two sons with two different men. One I married and one I did not, and I refused to have children with my new husband despite his strong desire. That's another emotional nightmare. We were divorced after a year of marriage. Nelson was killed after our divorce when he fell asleep behind the wheel of his car.

My life was taking a toll on everyone around me, including my children. I was overweight (5'2" and 186 lbs) with adult onset acne and was seriously fatigued. I suffered with intense shingles attacks and allergies and arthritis in my hands so bad I couldn't grip a glass. I had skin cancer, and my cervix was mutilated (as one doctor described it) with stage III dysphasia pre-cancer. Not to mention that I was diagnosed with PTSD, Borderline Personality Disorder, and Disassociative Personality Disorder, better known as Multiple Personality Disorder. This is another whole journey in itself. I was told I could never heal these disorders and that I would have to learn how to manage them. Words fail to describe the level of pain and despair I was experiencing during this period of my life.

I also needed lots of attention from men to feed my addiction for physical sexual stimulation, not to mention my own damaged sense of self. I had an excess of sexual stimulation during my developmental years, being sexually abused at three different stages in my developmental growth. Unfortunately, I had sex with all the wrong men. I found I couldn't make love with a man I cared about, only with a man I didn't love, and then I could only have detached unemotional sex. At the time, I only knew how to be a sexual object. I never knew anything different.

My life was still a mess, and my health issues now started to show up more frequently. Somewhere in the middle of all this insanity I found my way to a support group for sexually abused women and was given a book called *'You Can Heal Your Life'*, by Louise L. Hay. At the time, I didn't believe my life was worth saving; however, it piqued my curiosity, because I thought I might help save my sons from the hell I was in and help them find a better way.

The wheels started turning and I figured I would do the best I could. I left traditional therapy, which helped me understand what had happened to me, and realized that I wasn't the only one who had faced these problems. I realized that in fact I wasn't crazy and that there was a reason for the insanity in my life. That's when I came up with the mantra – it may not be my fault, however, it sure as hell is my problem. I used that to help heal myself over the next 25 years.

Chapter 2
Inspiration for Change: James and Troy

"Cardio-energetics says that our capacity for and willingness to give love is at least if not more important than how much we are loved. It is not so much 'feeling loved' as 'loving others' that is the way of the healing heart."

— Pg. 226 The Heart's Code: Tapping the Wisdom and Power of Our Heart Energy

My heart was truly healed because of the love I have for my sons James and Troy. I could do for them what I could or would not do for myself at least at that time. James and Troy were also having difficulty with their bodies. James began to bear the brunt of my unstable life when I married Dennis. I could hide a lot of my pain when it was just he and I. However, once I married Dennis, my unresolved issues really began to show themselves. Troy though, suffered from the very beginning of his life. My introduction into the journey of healing and what I now call my inner navigational system comes out of their suffering and my desire to help them. I surely didn't do it for myself because, as far as I was concerned, I was a lost cause or "damaged goods", as one man told me. By the age of 24 I had tried unsuccessfully to kill myself three times. Then I realized that if I did manage to kill myself by attempting to escape my painful existence, it meant I would leave my two innocent boys with the people who abused me.

At this time, James had in a matter of three years, broken each of his arms twice. Three accidents were on the school playground, and the last time he was hit by a car and broke his arm for the fourth time, also shattering his femur. He was put in a full body cast for two months after a month of traction and then spent another couple of months in a wheel chair. I had to teach him to walk again, because I had no money and his insurance benefits had run out for physical therapy. Now, one perspective could be that James was just accident-prone. However, James didn't break any bones before I was married and has not broken any bones since I divorced Dennis. Another perspective is that the root cause of broken bones, according the work of Louise L. Hay I learned was that breaking bones represents "rebellion against authority" (pg. 20). James and I had lived on our own for the most part before I married Dennis. When I married Dennis, James was five and a half years old and my husband Dennis was six foot five. He had an extremely overbearing authoritarian demeanor, especially when he was drinking.

The day after Troy's two-month 'well baby checkup' he developed a blockage in his intestines. Six inches of his intestines had in less than 24 hours become gangrene. The root cause of many stomach problems is fear and there was plenty of fear in our home (Hay, pg. 86). Gangrene energetically represents drowning in a lack of joy (Hay, pg. 36).

Troy almost died from having six inches of his intestines surgically removed without atheistic because he was so small at two months old. The surgeons were worried that if Troy received too much anesthetic he would go into a coma. Dennis and I had to consent to this surgery without anesthetic. We were also told that if he did go into shock, the anesthesiologist would have to use anesthetic and risk putting him into a coma because he would definitely die from shock from receiving no anesthetic. He did go into shock and the anesthesiologist administered the anesthetic, which put him into a coma for a few days. I went to his room every morning and whispered, "I understand if you choose to go; however, if you stay I will make sure you are loved." He woke up on the third morning and I was never so grateful.

Less than a year later, Troy developed a septic infection in his ankle, and was given large doses of antibiotics intravenously at the house for 5 days. I had to leave every time because I couldn't handle watching the pain that Troy was experiencing, and my staying would have created more pain for Troy.

I could have cared less about my life at this time because I couldn't see a way out of hell for me. However, I did love my two boys and thought that the least I could do was to stay alive and do the best I could for them to have a better chance at life than I had. I began not believing in God at this time. It was one thing that I wasn't protected as a little girl, but it was quite another for James and Troy not to be protected and to be suffering right before me. At the time I thought if there was a God why weren't we being protected. Somewhere down deep in my heart though, I knew their physical ailments and pain were directly related to the insanity in our home.

Just before Troy turned two years old he developed asthma and by the time he was three he was taking quite a few drugs just to help him breathe. The day I left Troy's father was two days after his third birthday. I had attended an SIA meeting (sexual incest anonymous) the night before. I left the boys with Dennis, and the next morning I noticed a full hand print on Troy's face and asked what happened. He said, "Daddy hit me". I was already in therapy because of our home situation, and part of my issue was that Troy always had an asthma attack when he was left alone with Dennis – it was like he was scared to death if I left him alone with his father.

My therapist said if I ever noticed unexplained marks or bruises on James or Troy, I was to take them to the hospital and get documentation immediately. And that is exactly what I did the moment Dennis left for work. Before Dennis left, I asked what happened to Troy last night and he said, "Troy couldn't breathe and I smacked him on the face so that he would start breathing." When we got to the hospital the police were called and so was Child Family Services. A report was filed against Dennis. I was also told by the police to pack up some clothes and leave our home immediately for a safe place or they would file a report against me for placing my sons back into an unsafe environment. I took a picture of Troy's face that day so I would never forget what happened. This was the breaking point for me.

I began this healing journey because my children deserved a better life than the one I knew and this was the turning point for me. This was the incentive I needed to go down the road that led to this book. I didn't see it this way when I first began. Like everything new, you just have to start somewhere. So I started with Louise Hay's *Heal Your Life* and looked up asthma, it had a section for Babies and Children, and it read, "Fear of life. Not wanting to be here." The affirmation is "This child is safe and loved. This child is welcomed and cherished" (Hay, pg. 75). I thought to myself, this is worse than horrible. Dennis and I helped create this situation for my children. I then looked up other *dis-eases* within my own body and the root causes that were attributed to each in Hay's "little blue book", as it is affectionately referred to, and was thrown into a tailspin. I might have been destroyed and beyond help; however, Troy and James were not. Funny thing was that the book I was reading told me that I wasn't a lost cause either. I didn't expect that!

That's the day I started this journey and the work I do now today. Troy was three and James was eight and a half when Dennis and I separated. Even when separated we fought all the time and one day after listening to his father and me fight, Troy suffered a really awful asthma attack and I rushed him to his pediatrician. His lips were blue and I was terrified because the drugs were not working and he could not breathe. The doctor wanted me to take Troy straight to the hospital to put him into a breathing tent. He said that Troy was not going to have a normal childhood and his asthma would probably follow him into adulthood. I just couldn't accept that and I left his office and instead of taking him to the hospital I took Troy straight home. I really liked

15

his pediatrician and Troy had already been through two surgeries and had almost died from the first one. He was a frightened child who did not smile his whole first year of tender life. It broke my heart. James laughed and smiled all the time when he was that young. I hurt because Troy hurt.

I had had enough of medicine and doctors and I wouldn't accept this as his fate. It was one thing to accept my fate, but not my children's fate. I took Troy home and I did exactly what that *"little blue book"* instructed me to do. I worked everyday with Troy until he began to feel better and then I began to wean him off his meds. I kept his father separated from me because he was court ordered out of the house. I would not fight anymore with Dennis and we began to learn to communicate with each other. I told Troy how much I loved him and James and how I was going to demonstrate this by changing my life and theirs for the better. I kept reinforcing to Troy that he was safe and loved by his father and me. And, even though we couldn't live together, we loved him.

To help Troy I began mirror work with him. We'd sit on the floor and I'd put a long mirror down and sit behind him with my legs gently wrapped around him while he looked at himself in the mirror. I would ask him if he was mad. He replied, "Yes!" I would ask why he was so angry, and he would tell me. Then we would go a little deeper (as deep as one can go with a three year old; however, you'd be surprised at how much they feel and can communicate given a chance) until he was able to connect to his emotions.

Once Troy's emotions began moving, I kept asking him questions all the while gently asking him to share with me and look at himself in the mirror – into his own eyes. At three years old he didn't have any reservations and did exactly what I asked him to do. I just let him have his feelings. At the end I would ask him if he could look into the mirror and say, 'Troy I love you', right into his eyes, and he did and would smile. Within three months of doing this work, Troy came off of his medications and he has not had another asthma attack since. I was thrilled, and my curiosity was piqued. I knew from the work I did with Troy that there was a real way to heal and that now I had to give it a shot with my own life.

Chapter 3
Your Inner Navigational System

"Since the consciousness of scientists and physicians is so disease-oriented, most of the research so far has been conducted to gain more of an understanding of disease-producing mechanisms. It seems as logical, however, for us to turn our attention in the other direction and to say that positive emotions should have a healthily, life-supporting influence on the body."

*— Pg. 8 Creating Health:
How to Wake Up the Body's Intelligence*

I am always amazed at how much money we as a society spend attempting to understand how methods from outside the body are supposed to "fix, repair, and many times remove" what is going on the inside of the body. However, we don't put an equal amount if not more money into understanding how what's going on inside of a person is affecting their health and how we can use that information to heal our bodies without having to resort to invasive treatments and drugs.

I have learned that our body and feelings are part of our inner navigational system. The creative force underlying the Universe did not design us to suffer with *dis-eases* and in chronic pain without a purpose. The Divine gave us a system to recognize when we're going in the wrong direction against our highest good. My experiences have taught me that pain is God's way of directing us to health, happiness and our highest good.

On this planet we can experience a number of different types of traumas, injuries, losses and accidents, not to mention overwhelming levels of stress. Many people have also suffered from childhood neglect, abuse and abandonment issues. How a person ends up in pain is different for each one of us. The more pain in your life, the more off course from your soul's truth you are. Whether you are aware of this or not, pain is a tool that when listened to, helps guide a person towards their highest good. Just as a moth is drawn towards the light, people are drawn towards happiness. The difficulty is that we weren't taught this information or knowledge and we accepted that becoming an adult meant suffering with stress, pain and *dis-ease.* Just as at one time the most learned of men believed the earth was flat and the center of the universe.

My grandmother lost at least four of her siblings due to childhood *dis-eases* and it is because of medical science that this is no longer an issue in our country. Also, doctors, researchers and pharmaceutical companies have helped civilization eradicate much *dis-ease* that once had devastating effects. They have nearly eradicated *dis-eases* like polio, tuberculosis, cholera and whooping cough and have had a major impact on reducing many physical symptoms in our country. Yet, because of these advances, we have created a dependence on the medical system and the drugs that come from it. Many of the *dis-eases* people are suffering with today are chronic. Relief is not found because the root cause is on the inside not the outside.

We have designed and created guidance systems to help us navigate our roadways, waterways, and airspace. We have maps, compasses, and GPS systems and now our phones have navigational systems also. Yet, we have failed to consider that we are created with our own personal inner navigational system to help us navigate this life. At one time in my life I didn't believe this either. I felt lost and lonely, not to mention I was in so much pain and darkness I couldn't imagine that I was given a gift at birth to help guide me to health and happiness. Your inner navigational system is designed to help guide you in everyday choices and especially when you have lost your way. This system can also guide and maintain your vibrancy without ever falling victim to *dis-ease*.

Your navigational system has an early warning system built into it, which communicates by way of comparison of your soul's highest good and your ability to make choices to support your highest good. If your choice is in alignment with your soul's highest good you will experience happiness and joy. If your choices are not in alignment with your soul's highest good you will experience discomfort, pain and any number of sensations like headaches and heartburn to alert you that a choice is out of alignment. This gives you the opportunity to re-evaluate your choice(s). For example, you've just eaten dinner and afterwards you experience heartburn. Instead of just taking an antacid to reduce the symptoms, take the time to also ask yourself what created the heartburn? Was it really the food? Was it the company you shared while eating the food? Was it eating alone again? Was it how fast you devoured your food? Your highest good also may not be the same as the societal good, the church's idea of your highest good, or your family's idea of good, or even the ideas of the family you marry into. This system is designed to give you feedback about how you are going to be the happiest, period; not how happy everyone else around you will be.

We're given opportunities all day long to choose our highest good. Another example of not recognizing your highest good: you're asked to bake cookies for the church picnic and before you realize it, you feel your insides cringe and draw tight. You want to say 'no', and yet you say, "Yes, I'd be happy to!" Your soul wants you to choose your highest good, speak up for yourself and say that you already have too much on your plate. Try this instead, "Thank you for asking, maybe next time I will have time to help." Your highest good at this moment is to save all the energy you can to take care of your family given that many of us have experienced the children being home from school sick, your husband or wife working overtime the last couple of weeks and your parents are living with you because they need help in their aging years all at the same moment.

Once you've said yes and walked away, you may begin to ruminate on the fact that you really don't have time to bake cookies. You might "feel" a cold coming on or an upset stomach or a headache. Some people will even make themselves sick so they can create a good excuse for pulling out at the last minute, instead of just being able to listen to your own body and feel whether this is something you're truly able to do. The same holds true for men; however, their choices are made from a different definition of importance. They also overextend themselves, generally in work, sports and projects at home, without being able to hear their internal navigational system, which creates pain and *diseases* in their bodies.

My journey has taught me that healing and staying pain free does take a commitment to learning how to listen to your body and emotions as a navigational system. To find a connection with this internal system you have to slow your world down so you can hear your body's subtle cues and messages. When you use any drugs, whether illicit (marijuana, cocaine, and other people's prescription drugs) or legal (alcohol, prescription pain killers and cigarettes, etc.), you alter your body's signals and drown out what it is attempting to communicate to you. Shopping, overeating and gambling are socially acceptable activities we abuse to ignore our feelings and our pain. The list of activities we use is extensive given there are many ways to ignore our feelings and drown out our pain.

As children grow into mature adults, we have no idea how much conditioning is used to shut off their navigational system. Ever since our childhood years our socialization process has helped us disregard our navigational system. When you were young and you were hungry, you would cry or maybe even scream until you were fed. When a small child doesn't like someone, they naturally pull back and have no problem at first telling them no. When a child is tired they go to sleep. Yet, as we get older, we are taught to ignore our inner promptings so that we can fit into society and its norms. As a child, your highest good was listened to; as an adult your highest good is mainly ignored. As a person grows and matures and takes on more responsibilities, stress begins to take a toll on the mind, the body and spirit. Your soul wants you to hear the cry of pain as an indicator that you are off-track from your highest good and are going in the wrong direction.

Chapter 4
Your Inner Traffic Light

"The individual's health fails when he or she experiences a powerful unhappiness in life. The source of the problem may be work, school, family life, romance, or athletics. To avoid feeling pain, he or she tries to ignore the problem by focusing on other things thus becoming unaware that the situation is eating away at him or her."

— Pg. 5 When Chicken Soup is Not Enough:
Revolutionary Healing Though the
Mind-Body Connection

When we are unaware that a situation is troubling us in some way, our bodies begin to let us know, and when we are able to listen to our bodies and our feelings, they will give us direction. The more unconscious a person is to their pain, the louder the body will scream. God gave us the ability to find our way to happiness and living a pain free life by listening to our inner navigational system.

This system has a guidance method similar to the traffic light we all use everyday to navigate the traffic on our streets. When your inner light is green everything in your life flows. You do not experience bumps and bruises, scratches or accidents. Your body is pain free and you are vibrant and full of energy. Your life unfolds before you and is lived with joy and happiness. You love the work you do and look forward to getting up and out of bed in the morning, versus hitting the snooze button again and again just to get another moment of sleep. You look forward to the day and the opportunities that await you. If you drop something you are able to catch it before it hits the ground. You don't hit your funny bone or run into furniture. Life is smooth. You have boundaries and yet are free and open to enjoy life and those around you.

When your inner light turns yellow and you are cognizant of this information, you will notice a change in your emotional and physical body. You may notice that you're a little tired and irritable. You may get a headache, stomachache or any number of little irritations, like your lower back hurting. Other yellow light indications are the small burns from the oven or toaster. You may get cuts and scratches and little annoying skin inflammations. Bugs and insects biting you like mosquitoes, wasps, bees and hornets, not to mention hitting your funny bone, and it is less than funny. These experiences are all to be found within the realm of your inner navigational light being yellow. When your body is overworked and screaming at you to take some time for yourself and you don't, you may catch a cold, the flu or a stomach virus. Upper respiratory infections are also common when a person is not listening to their body and overextending him or herself. Included in this list, but not limited to, are acne, asthma, arthritis, broken bones allergies, and skin aliments such as psoriasis and eczema. High blood pressure and cholesterol are also in the realm of the yellow light.

This is a brief list of how our bodies begin to communicate with us. By the time the light is yellow a person has ignored these messages and is unable to hear the more subtle clues their body and feelings were attempting to share. This system is set up so that your body begins to get your attention that your choices do not support your highest good. Pain and *dis-ease* is one of the ways in which God designed our bodies to communicate with us in an attempt to get our attention. Many of us believe we are too busy to take the time to ask ourselves why we're in pain, so instead we just go to the doctor's office. I have found that doctors on occasion can help reduce the pain and symptoms in the short term for many stress related *dis-eases*. However, when the root cause of the pain is not addressed, with time, the same pain generally returns or the pain can become more pronounced.

When driving, and the traffic light turns yellow, it means yield, slow down, and pay attention to possible oncoming traffic. The same could be said about our body. Instead of slowing down and paying attention to traffic, the inner yellow light demands that a person slow down and pay attention to the body with questions and introspection. Most people are taught that when you're ill or not feeling well then it is time to go to the doctor. In our allopathic health care system, doctor's assistants or nurses generally check your vitals, take blood if needed and ask questions about what kind of symptoms you're exhibiting. At this point the doctor enters and without asking any questions that delve into what is going on in your personal and work life and the choices you are making that may have lead to creating the presenting symptoms he or she addresses the symptomatology. Many physicians are not trained to look for the underlying root causes of pain. They are trained to help relieve the symptoms only, so they give you a prescription and may set you up for a round of tests. However, in recent years there has been a movement of physicians who are embracing the idea that the body has a natural healing system of it's own and they are there to support this process.

So now we're up to the color red on your inner traffic light. Red means a person is in trouble because the next level after red is dead. When a person refuses to or does not realize they have the power to wake up out of their denial and choose their highest good by assuming responsibility for their life and their choices, the body can deteriorate into pain and suffering. At this level a person is probably suffering with a lot of pain and discomfort, and has been to many doctors, or to the hospital numerous times. The doctors and their staff will run tests, poke and prod, and yet people are generally still left in pain long after they've left the hospital

The *dis-eases* in red are life threatening or extremely debilitating, such as heart disease, cancer, type II diabetes and mental illness. A person may also experience a life altering tragic accident. Like all traffic lights, red comes after yellow, and red means stop and immediately look at your life and choices and beliefs. Red means your life is compromised. Louise L. Hay's writes in her book *Heal Your Life*, the word 'incurable' emotional root cause; "Cannot be cured by outer means at this point. We must go within to effect a cure. It came from nowhere and it will go back to nowhere." (Pg. 43.)

Generally, when a person's red light is activated, they are in a lot of pain emotionally and physically. They are general fatigued and can be challenged in any number of ways. A person whose red light is activated can still do this work and recover fully because the depth of their discomfort may be the inspiration they needed to change and grow. However, it is much easier if you are able to begin this work before you get to red.

Unfortunately, the way our medical system is set up a person can be in "red" for a number of years without the hope of healing. This is what I term 'the walking dead', where a person is still alive and yet they have no quality of life at all, because they suffer an enormous amount of pain and so they take lots of prescriptions drugs and pain medication in order to ease the symptoms and discomfort of their *'dis-ease'*.

People pray to God to get them out of pain, and yet I have experienced and found that the Divine already gave us the power to get out of pain. The Divine gave you the power of choice. This is similar to the story I was told years ago about God helping, and how we don't realize the Divine is always helping us. As the story goes, 'it had rained for days in this little town and rescue crews were sent to help the townspeople who were stranded and couldn't get to higher ground. A man was on top of his roof when a canoe came by and the man in the canoe said,' "Get in and I'll take you to higher ground." "'The man on the roof said, '"No, I'm waiting on God to save me."'" As the stranded man waited the water level rose higher and a bigger boat came to save the man. The man in the bigger boat said, "Get in, I'll take your to higher ground," and once again the man on the roof said, "'No, I'm waiting for God to save me.'" Now the water was up to the roof and the biggest boat of all came by, and once again man on the roof was asked to get in the boat. Once again, the man said, "'No, I'm waiting for God to save me.'" Well, the man drowned, and when he came before God he asked, "God why didn't you save me?" God replied, "'I tried three times, but you didn't get in the boat!'" God can only help you when you choose to help yourself.

This can be a hard concept for many people to grasp given the way we have been 'helped' by western medicine and science. Yet, there are many things that science and medicine cannot answer and there are many things they have been wrong about in the past. That is not to say that western medicine hasn't advanced us and helped us live better healthier lives. However, God did give us the ability to help ourselves also. We were given the power of free will and the ability to choose our highest good. And yet we want to pick and choose when this applies and when it doesn't. You are at all times responsible for your life; you are made in the image of God. People and everything in the universe are part of the creative life force. People are given the gift and power of co-creating with the Divine at all times whether you are aware of this fact or not. It's like gravity just because you're ignorant of it doesn't mean it's not working on you. This knowledge is what gave me the power to change my life. I have taken responsibility for my life by being responsible for my choices, thoughts and feelings. When a person is out of alignment with their soul and chooses to make anyone else happy at their expense, it will always show up as pain in their body. When you follow your heart's desire and listen to your body, you will be pain free and able to experience joy and happiness during your own life's journey.

Chapter 5
How To Reclaim Your Connection to Your Inner Navigational System

"Grace illuminates your path by moving through your intuition, influencing the choices that you make. When left to our own devices, we often choose to do things that reflect our shadow side-the dark fears and uncertainty about our ability to survive in the physical world. Nonetheless, we always have an awareness, a feeling, or a gut instinct about what we should think, say or do. When we say, 'I don't know what to do,' we are rarely being truthful."

— Pg. 17 Invisible Acts of Power: Personal Choices The Create Miracles

It isn't enough to want to reconnect with your inner voice and awareness. As with anything new, a person needs to practice listening to their inner voice and the awareness that is always available to us. Being able to reconnect to the innate knowledge that is contained within each of us of is accessible to everyone. When young, most children eat when they are hungry, sleep when they are tired and fully express their feelings no matter who is around. As children begin to grow and experience more of life, they have a tendency not to listen to their inner guidance, that inner voice of knowing.

As we grow and develop, the voices we choose to listen to are the voices of our family and the church we attend with our families. Peer pressures begin from the time we are little until we die to fit into society and adopt their values. We hear their voices and we also hear the advertising we are bombarded with daily. Not to mention, our teachers and bosses. We get in the habit of listening to everyone outside of ourselves and begin to ignore the voice inside. Habits begin to control the reactions of our bodies as we routinely deny our inner voice. Habits are learned behaviors of externalizing and generalizing approved rules of behavior, which override our natural responses to people and situations.

We begin to lose touch with our inner voice early in life because we are socialized and taught how to fit into our culture and society. Our parents, families, churches and schools all have standards that we are taught to maintain, and it is believed that this is for our greatest good. However, no one except you knows what is best for your highest and greatest good. We lose touch with our navigational system because, without even realizing it, we stopped listening to our truth in favor of listening to someone else's truth. We made choices to do things we didn't want to do because at the beginning of our lives we had no power to make different choices, or we made the choice to ignore our feelings initially because of a bigger payoff: getting onto a particular sports team, or fitting in with certain groups, or having our mom or dad approve of us. Given that the list of people to listen to can be so exhaustive; we ultimately learn to listen to the outside messages, instead of the messages from inside. On the other hand, deep within your being, behind every choice before you, beneath every idea or want there is a voice within you to be heard. This voice knows and communicates exactly what is best for you in any given situation. This voice is so subtle you must become quiet and still to detect its presence, and yet when you're able to hear this voice you will be able to respond appropriately to situations and circumstances in the best way for you in that moment.

Even if we're able to make it out of childhood happy and joyful and still listening to our inner voice, we can sometimes lose touch with our inner voice in our adult lives. Learning how to be able to balance our lives with work, getting married and having children is another instance when we don't make the time to listen to this voice. Most of us keep up with cleaning the home, the yard, cooking meals, shopping, earning enough money for bills and paying them, retirement, college tuition for the children and countless other activities. This is not even to mention the energy it takes to keep up with the children, pets, after school activities, church and church activities, family gatherings, and birthdays, etc. The inability to moderate the stress in our lives can help to create *dis-ease*.

Unfortunately, many other children lose the ability to listen to their inner voice due to being traumatized as a child. A child that is traumatized and/or abused in any way during childhood and is not given the opportunity to express their truth with honesty and confront their feelings, will shut down this system for survival. Children cannot feel that much pain without their internal system shutting down to preserve themselves. Many times a child who is traumatized can suppress feelings and pain in their body for decades.

Health and vitality are natural. The symptoms in your body give you clues along the way to help you find those causes for the imbalances. Allow your body to release deep feelings. You may need someone along the way to help you release these feelings and process them. Here are a few words that accompanied me on my journey towards healing and may help you as you're learning to listen to your body. The words I utilized on my healing journey have become my best friends. They are: Courage, faith, trust, surrender, acceptance, love, compassion, patience, support, boundaries, and, most of all, forgiveness.

To reconnect with your inner navigational system you have to learn to listen to your body and love it. When you ache, give your pain your full attention. Rather than running to the doctor or pharmacy and getting drugs to block the pain and using over the counter or prescribed medication's talk with the pain. Just stop and take a moment. Listen to it and ask why it is there. In the beginning, especially if a person is truly suffering with pain, this may be easier said than done. However, if you truly want to get out of pain there is a way. Bodywork with the right person can help find places in your body where there are imbalances and help you reconnect with your body, your feelings, and your inner voice.

Assess your situation and lifestyle. What are you doing to yourself and for yourself? If you are tired, do you rest? What kind of food does your body need? We are all different. Foods that work for another person may not work for you.

How much water do you drink? Do you consistently eat junk food, smoke, and use large amounts of caffeine and alcohol just to get through the day? Do you love the work you do for a living or is it just a way to make money? To be healthy, you may be required to change your job, not to mention change your relationships, friends, habits, and lifestyle. Whatever needs to be addressed, your body will let you know if you are willing to slow down and take the time to listen. I used to believe that I didn't have time to slow down and listen; however, I am vibrant and full of energy today because of slowing down and listening to my body. Now I have more than enough energy and time to accomplish everything I want and need to do. It takes more time out of a day to suffer with pain, go to the doctors, to be miserable and have no energy, than to listen to inner knowing; just as it takes more facial muscles to create a frown than to smile. It's efficient to be happy and well. As the saying in my studio goes, when you're sick and tired of being sick and tired, you'll find a way to hear your truth.

Chapter 6
The Toxic Wasteland

"Your body is your creation. It tells you what is working and what isn't. At birth, most of us were given a beautiful, vital body, sustained by the natural free flow of the universal energy. Look how tireless and spontaneous young children are. They eat when hungry, sleep when tired, and fully express their feelings. As life experiences leave their impression, negative habits develop . . . Chronic negative behaviors are reflected in the body as aches and pains, fatigue and minor illness. When you don't notice, these signals then get stronger until there is a serious or fatal result."

— *Pg. 43 Angel Blessings*

When we are young our bodies are generally light and free. As we experience life and age and are unaware of how to release stress properly, our bodies begin to become heavy and bound, tightening and drawing inward. We are no longer open and free. Many people believe this is a natural process of aging. I disagree. I have come to believe it is a natural process of ignoring our passion for life and our

Divine life purpose. We will all age, yet people don't have to grow old and fall into disrepair. After years of ignoring and denying how you are really feeling, your body can turn into a painful toxic wasteland. This is one of the reasons it can take people a while to clear out the toxic feelings and habits from the body once they've chosen to clean it out. It all depends on how much of your feelings and truth you've denied, ignored and pushed down deep inside of you.

Most children are free and clear of physical and emotional baggage in the beginning. If you were allowed as a child to acknowledge your feelings at the time they occurred and worked through them, they will not be carried forward in the physical body. However, that is generally not what occurs. Most children by the age of four have been spanked and scared into behaving properly by the people they love and depend on to care for them. Many times children are yelled at for being too loud or excited when they are just having fun. And many children are told to stop crying and 'suck it up'. The energy of fear, anger, hurt, abandonment, and any other negative feelings they have are stuffed away and pushed down deep into the belly. This becomes the ground floor of what I call your toxic waste dump. Every single time after the first initial hurt that is left unfelt and is denied, suppressed, ignored or is pushed down inside the body, the layers get thicker and thicker. Many of us also add in unhealthy foods, sugar, preservatives, drugs and alcohol, without drinking plenty of water or sleeping well. Next, add loads of stress and an unhealthy lifestyle, and over the years more and more layers are added into this intangible wasteland.

It's similar to a kitchen trash compactor, where the more recent trash will be easier to remove because it isn't as tightly pushed down and compacted as the trash is in the middle and at the bottom. Depending on how long the trash ferments, it will contribute to the smell and density of the trash in the compactor. The same analogy can be made with your body and your feelings. The most recent uncomfortable feelings or situations can be healed far easier than the ones buried deep inside, most times hidden from conscious awareness.

Aging can exacerbate pain, especially when the pain has been ignored, denied or anesthetized for a number of years. What our bodies can handle when we are young and what our bodies can handle as we age are two very different things. When you're twenty and you injure your body, you can recover incredibly quickly as opposed to having the same injury at fifty or sixty not to mention at seventy or eighty. The point is that physical bodies can hold feelings of anger, resentment, jealousy, bitterness, guilt and shame when we're in our 20's, and we can choose to deny, ignore or suppress our feelings because we are physically strong and these feelings generally aren't strong enough to override the body's physical strength, unless the trauma is deep and severe. Yet, as we age, our bodies are not as strong and we are unable to keep these feelings and emotions buried any longer and they begin to create *dis-ease* to get our awareness.

We choose not to address the underlying root cause of our pain because of a bigger payoff. When you're young, the payoff of making more money, even though you may hate your job or boss, is not so painful. The same goes for an unhappy marriage or any of the choices we make and live with when our bodies are young. However, as we age the

41

pain starts to outweigh the payoffs, and we have developed a habit of ignoring our pain until it is chronic and unbearable. Or we have developed a life threatening *dis-ease* because our once vibrant healthy bodies are filled with toxic feelings and pain. There is a way to clear out the toxic feelings and pain that create the *dis-ease* in our bodies. Today there are a number of books to help a person discover their way. Some of my guides are Louise L. *Hay's Heal Your Body* and *You Can Heal Your Life,* which at the time, were the only guides I was aware of that could help guide me into my body and begin to learn to feel my feelings and understand their connection to the pain in my body. Both *Feelings Buried Alive – Never Die . . .* by Karol K. Truman and *When Chicken Soup Isn't Enough: Revolutionary Healing Through the Mind-Body Connection* by Dr. Ralph Rutherford are other great resources. Over the years, I have come to experience and learn that the body does not lie – we lie to ourselves.

Chapter 7
Your Tangible and Intangible Bodies

"We want to use a holistic approach. The holistic philosophy is to nurture and nourish the entire being – the body, the mind, and the spirit. If we ignore any of these areas, we are incomplete, we lack wholeness. It doesn't matter where we start as long as we also include the other areas."

— *Pg. 88. You Can Heal Your Life*

I f you are anything like me, you were taught you have one body. Yet I have come to discover we have five different bodies. One tangible solid physical body and four intangible ethereal bodies, and all have to be cared for if we are to be whole and healthy. Your tangible body is your physical body, the one you can perceive through the sense of touch. The remaining four intangibles are: the emotional, psychological, sexual and spiritual bodies. These can only be perceived by feeling. You cannot touch or see your intangible bodies. However, they will certainly let you know they are there, if you begin to pay attention. Just like your five senses, they give you information all the time to help guide you in making choices that bring your highest good, happiness and joy. The problem is that most of us have been trained to listen to the opinions of others. And, similar to me, at some point in your life you may have felt like your body betrayed you. I experienced this as a small child being sexually molested by men I loved and trusted. I was terrified out of my mind and yet my body would orgasm from the stimulation. I chose at a very young age to stop paying attention to what my body was experiencing and numb my feelings. Nevertheless, you don't have to be a child to experience feeling like your body has betrayed you. As an adult you can feel as though your body has betrayed you when, seemingly out of nowhere, you have a stroke, or are told you have cancer, Parkinson's, or any number of *dis-eases*.

These intangible 'bodies' at first communicate with us through feelings. If we don't believe feelings have the power to communicate or if we choose not to hear our feelings by ignoring them and numbing ourselves to them, then we feel the subtle communication from the intangible bodies which use the physical body to send messages known as discomfort, pain and *dis-ease* to get our awareness.

Your emotional body has an enormous effect on your physical body and the health and happiness you experience in your life. For example, even the most skeptical person and most doctors will agree that 'stress' can make a person very ill and ultimately kill them. One emotional experience many people have felt is having their heart broken. The one you love is not longer in love with you. Another emotional experience many people have experienced is finding out that the person you have shared your most intimate being with is going behind your back and betraying your trust on some level. Feelings are an internal emotional experience, and yet at the same time they can be felt on a physical level. They can have very physical effects like insomnia, depression, heartburn and the list goes on. And yes, I have read and heard that it is only a chemical reaction. I was a complete disbeliever at one time of teachers and body workers who recommended that if I began to work with my feelings, my body would begin to heal.

Psychological distress, better known as mental stress, can also show up as illness in the physical body and take a toll on a person's health. Many people lost their jobs after the financial crisis of 2008. A large segment of the workforce that was laid off was between the ages of 30 and 50. Also, during this time, many graduating college students were left with college debt without the ability to secure employment and had to move back home with mom and dad. Anxiety and fear can immediately set in as well as thoughts like, 'what am I going to do now? How are the bills going to get paid? Will I be able to get a new job?' Such thoughts begin to overrun the mind. Other psychological stresses many couples can identify with are those of staying in toxic marriages. Some do this for financial reasons, some for the sake of the children, and all at the expense of their health. Many times there is an emotional element to psychological distress.

The sexual body often has feelings of its own, and many people, whether they recognize it or not, have an innate sexual drive that is extremely personal and unique to him or her. We are all sexual beings whether we choose to have sex or not. This is separate from sexual organs. The way you have been taught about your sexuality has an affect on your long term overall health. Whether a person embraces their sexuality or denies his or her sexuality can have an effect on their physical body. Many children experience sexual and physical abuse. The numbers of girls and boys that are sexually abused before the age of sixteen is frightening. In addition, how a child is raised whether in an conservative, liberal, orthodox or extremely open religious family atmosphere and how these ideas harmonize with the child's inner knowing about their own sexuality can have an effect on their health as they mature, develop and get married. Both the church and family can affect how an adult, much less a developing teenager, feels and thinks about their sexuality. Something as simple as being taught to masturbate and enjoy the body versus hiding or being punished for masturbating has a dramatic effect on a person's physical health. Even more important are all the countless ways we've been taught or not taught about sex.

I can tell you from my life's work that many people with migraine headaches are hard driving and either internally criticize themselves or have a need to release sexual tension. (Hay. pg. 49). Without doubt, a person has to rule out any organic reasons for the headaches first. However, if there is nothing organically wrong and a person is still experiencing migraine headaches, it generally clears up when a person begins to slow down internally and begins to have regular sexual activity. This helps release built up energy and stress whether the sex is by himself or herself or with a loving partner.

Spiritually and religiously accepting a belief system that does not resonate with your own inner truth can create pain and *dis-ease* in a person's body. Accepting without critical consideration the views your family has always believed, may conflict with your spiritual body. You may have this nagging feeling within you that your inner truth conflicts with what you are being taught. Many times we don't question what doesn't feel right and accept as truth what we're taught. It is said that you have to 'take it on faith' whether it feels wrong or not. - Earlier, I mentioned questioning Sister Mary Ann, "Why would I go to hell just because my family members had sex with me?" It didn't feel right and I was punished for wanting to question the church and its leadership while looking for an answer within that resonated with MY soul.

When we accept someone else's truth or viewpoint on faith without taking the time to find out what is actually true for us, whether it's in our emotional, psychological sexual or spiritual body, we can be taken off course from our soul's journey and truth. Always find the source. This is where your navigational system helps guide you back to homeo-stasis – balance within yourself. On the ancient temple of Delphi it read, "Know thy self" and this stills holds true today.

Chapter 8
The Responsibility of Free Will

"Now is the time to acknowledge our responsibility in having created the situation or condition. I'm not talking about having guilt, nor about being a 'bad person' for being where you are. I am saying to acknowledge the 'power within you' that transforms our every thought into experience. In the past we unknowingly used this power to create things we did not want to experience. We were not aware of what we were doing. Now, by acknowledging our responsibility, we become aware and learn to use this power consciously in positive ways for our benefit."

— Pg. 56 You Can Heal Your Life

Human beings are given a most powerful gift called free will – the ability to choose. Many people do not realize what a powerful tool they have to work with every day, all day. From the moment a child is born this gift is present. How this tool is utilized as we mature into adults is considerably different from person to person because of the ability to choose and the differences in which we are all raised. Many people blame others or the way they were raised for their inability to choose well for themselves. I was one of those people.

As a teenager, with many violent family circumstances hitting me all at once, I somehow chose to believe I was worthless and the cause of these events. Many people will ask how I could have known better. This is hard for people and many will disagree with me on this point, because I know I did for the longest time. We have free will to choose from the moment we take our first breath. Free will doesn't just show up at some given age. Now, as a child, we may not have the ability to choose all things for ourselves, however, we do have the ability to choose how we feel about ourselves and what we believe in. Instead of choosing to believe that other family members created these situations, I chose to believe that I was the cause of these experiences. I could have chosen to believe in my innate connection with God and myself and yet I didn't; I chose to believe my family's version of the truth. No matter what life circumstance a person finds himself or herself in, he or she always has the ability to choose his or her highest good. The word "responsibility" refers to the ability to respond. How a person responds is their choice, and with all choices come consequences.

Pain is an incredible teacher. A teacher can teach you how to be in the world or how not to be in the world. Pain is the same - the greater your pain, the louder your navigational system becomes in an effort to get your attention. Pain is the universe's way of getting your attention so that you may become conscious of your choices and the need to choose differently to find your way to happiness and joy. This includes self-love and forgiving others who have harmed you in the past. Your navigational system warns you when you are not choosing well for yourself or holding on to past hurts. This is how I've healed my life.

I teach yoga as a practice, and I now apply this approach to my entire life. Life is a practice. Remembering how to listen to your navigational system is a practice, and it takes time and effort. You have to remember that you have a system and then learn (or relearn) how to use it. This takes faith and trust in yourself and your Creator. The Divine never left me, I chose to leave God. When you came into this life, God had a Divine purpose for your soul's journey, and you chose to be where you are to fulfill that Divine purpose by using your free will and choice to experience this journey. You are a spiritual being having a human experience, and you were given the gift of free will and choice to help you create your journey. Quoting Gary Zukav, "Try to realize, and truly realize, that what stands between you and a different life are matters of responsible choice." (Zukav, pg. 25). To paraphrase what Gary said; what stands between you and vibrant health are really matters of responsible choice.

Louise L. Hay's work teaches that if you're not being responsible with your choices then you're blaming others for your choices. (Hay, pg. 56). And there are so many things we blame for our pain and *dis-ease*. We blame our mothers and fathers. We blame our ex-wives and husbands. We blame our children. We blame society, genetics and nature. We blame our lack of money. We blame our job, bosses and the economy. We blame our teachers. We blame our inability to get to the proper medical facility. We blame our doctors, the hospital and insurance companies. We blame the government, and many of us even blame God. We blame anyone and everyone except ourselves for our choices or lack of choices. And yet, as I discussed earlier, we are given the ability to choose and create our lives and live in joy and happiness no matter what life throws in our direction.

People cannot understand why they are in pain and have no energy. And yet, if you look at most people who complain of the minor aches and pains of life, they are individuals who choose everyday to ignore basic health needs. Examples of this is: Not drinking enough water every day, (sleeping at least six hours every night, although a good night's sleep is more like eight hours of uninterrupted sleep. Not tossing and turning because you can't go to sleep), eating healthy foods and staying away from processed foods and sugar, making time for touch and intimate conversation with other people, having sex regularly and taking time each day to be still and just relax and breathe.

My life is a living testament that even the most mangled life can be healed when one stops 'blaming' and starts taking responsibility for one's own choices, thoughts, feelings and attitude. Anyone who has the determination was given the power within to heal his or her life. It's work. Take allergies for instance. We blame nature. People believe as I did and we have been taught, that the reason for our allergies is that our bodies are having an adverse reaction to something out there, whether it is pollution, pollen, dust, food or cats. You name it and people are allergic to it. Allergies affect millions of people every year.

For many years I suffered with terrible allergies. Sometimes my eyes would swell up so bad I couldn't open them. I used a bath towel for a tissue at times because my nose ran so much. Laying down would cause my sinuses to fill up with mucous and when I wasn't using a bath towel, I would go through boxes of Kleenex daily. Most of the time during the spring and fall I was beyond miserable. I would be so irritated with my body for reacting to pollen and ragweed to the point that I felt allergies controlled my life. The drugs I took only made things worse. My mouth would dry out, or I would get so sleepy I couldn't stay awake or some drugs would speed me up inside.

When I got miserable enough, I looked up allergies in my little blue book and it read, 'Who are you allergic to?' 'Denying your own power.' It didn't say what you could be allergic to. I began to answer the question who am I allergic to. And I found the answer bothered me, because it was mostly people closest to me. When I addressed the statement 'denying my own power' relating to the choices I was making, and then started to make other choices to empower myself, it sure did upset the balance in my family and my circle of friends.

People around me became uncomfortable because I changed the way I perceived the world and those around me. I began to be responsible for the way I felt, the choices I made and the people I spent time with. I also began to use the book's affirmation: 'the world is safe and friendly. I am safe. I am at peace with life.'

For the last 15 years I have been allergy free, no matter where I go in the world or what time of the year. No drugs, no therapies, no doctors, no shots. Just a real understanding of my body communicating with me that I didn't feel safe with certain people and that I ultimately had the power to make the changes I needed to feel safe in the world.

Many people do not want to do the inner work and admit that they're denying their own internal power by not addressing who is irritating them in their life or not going deeper to look within themselves for the answers and the solutions. Most people would much rather blame someone or something outside himself or herself. It seems so much easier than looking within for the answers to why we do not feel well, not to mention all the other reasons we use to make excuses for the lack of health in our bodies.

Perhaps the experience of one of my students will help demonstrate the common challenges in addressing the responsibility of free will.

Vivian age 46

"I have never had a way with words, but here it goes...

Today in class our word for the day was - love, which is another thing that I have never been very good at. My entire adult life has been riddled with sickness including Fibromyalgia, IBS, allergies, asthma, and insomnia. I have panic and anxiety disorder. Over half of my income in my lifetime has been handed over to doctors or therapists trying to "fix" me. I finally found a wonderful physician that suggested that I try yoga. One day while driving, I noticed a sign "Mountain Yoga and Healing". So I decided to call once I returned home. I spoke with Donna Marie; she suggested I start with a few private sessions since I had never taken yoga and was in a lot of pain. When I came to Donna Marie, I was a real mess! I was a chain smoker in very poor health. I had bronchitis for several months, and was experiencing daily panic attacks. Even though I had never taken yoga, I just knew that she was not your typical yoga instructor. I knew right away that we were a good fit! Donna Marie showed me compassion. She showed me that she really believes in what she is doing. Together we are finding the tools that work for me, to heal me. She works one on one with all her students, because not all people are the same. Each and every one in her class has their own special need. She takes time in every class to ask each student if they have a special need, or a certain ailment that she may need to address. My love tank was empty, and my fear tank was overflowing when I walked into this studio. I made an appointment with hypnotherapist Karen Perleoni, who also works out of the studio, to help calm my anxiety. I have been attending classes with Donna Marie on a weekly basis. It's now been eight months, and I have moved from a beginner's class to a beginner's step-up class. I have minimal flare-ups of Fibromyalgia, my bronchitis has disappeared entirely, and I have my anxiety under - control. I have also stopped smoking cigarettes. Mountain Yoga and Healing has helped me to put a plug in my fear tank. Thank you to my fellow classmates for all of your encouragement. My love tank is starting to fill. Now I just can't wait for my appointment with Melissa Garland for my reflexology session!"

This is one of the many reasons why I love doing the work I do; helping others find their way out of pain and begin to find their way back to their highest good and happiness. It is a true experience of joy and happiness for me and has brought tremendous meaning and purpose to my life.

Chapter 9
The Hardest Step: Change

"It has become apparent to me that assuming that everyone wants to heal is both misleading and potentially dangerous. Illness can, for instance, become a powerful way to get attention you might not otherwise receive – as a form of leverage, illness can seem attractive. Illness may also convey the message that you have to change your life quite drastically. Because change is among the most frightening aspects of life, you may fear change more intensely than illness and enter into a pattern of postponing the changes you need to make."

— Pg ix Why People Don't Heal and How They Can

One of the hardest steps in healing your life is making changes and then following through with them, especially when change not only affects your life but the people closest to you. Most of us don't like change; however, we don't mind change as much if the changes only affect us. On the other hand, when change is going to affect others, we have to talk with people around us and let them know we're in the process of changing our own lives. This can bring about a lot of defensive emotions like fear, anger, and abandonment issues. Remember, though, that our issues are generally tied in with the people in our lives. Most people don't like change and won't approve of you changing your life if it affects their lives.

If you're in chronic pain, your body is attempting to get your attention to change your choices and align yourself with your highest good; this will surely impact those who share your life. If you're not comfortable with change, the people you've chosen to be in relationship with probably aren't all that comfortable with change either.

I had a student who drank for over 25 years to numb her pain from being abused sexually, emotionally and psychologically. She finally decided to change, and said 'enough is enough.' Her family did want her to stop drinking. They felt if she would just stop drinking things would get better. They were willing and accepting for her to make that change. Well, she stopped drinking and began to do yoga with me at the studio. She had wanted to do yoga for quite a while and knew she had to stop drinking before she could begin my class, and she did. She began to really change, because she could now think clearly. She didn't need to be told what to do, and suddenly it began to cause conflict in her family. She had a desire to dress more youthfully, wearing brighter more vibrant colors. However, it scared her husband, which then trickled down to her adult children. She began to assert herself about what she wanted to do differently to be happy. Her family didn't like that she drank; however, they were suddenly not comfortable with her newfound happiness and their inability to control her newfound freedom to be herself. They got angry with her and created so many stressful situations that she found herself wanting to drink again. I hear from some of the people I've worked with that it's just not worth it. And unfortunately, so it is with her, at least at this point in time.

When it becomes apparent that certain aspects of your life to which you have become accustomed are dramatically shaken up and begin to fall away, your ability to undergo these difficult transitions will demonstrate to you where your doubts and fears reside. In fact, it is an inevitable part of the journey to dismantle the old and clear a path for the new. The truth is that you may very well lose your marriage, members of your family and even - leave your job. Sometimes change requires you to leave the life you once knew, as I needed to do. I had to completely change the way I was living in order to find what truly made me happy. The ties to my family and friends were too strong for me to make the changes I needed to reclaim my life. Not everyone has to go to this extreme to recreate his or her life. My life is an extreme example and helps illustrate the ability that we all have within ourselves to heal. I am of the belief that if I could heal from my life experiences then anyone can heal, from the smallest of discomfort to overwhelming devastation and destruction. Since healing my life, I have worked on new ways of relating to my family and have developed a new circle of friends who continue to support me in my healing journey. It is amazing to anyone who goes on this journey how much resistance one can receive from those who say they love you. If they truly love you and you give them the time to adjust to your changes, they will embrace your happiness and come around. Or they will leave. If they leave, it is truly for your highest good.

Chapter 10
The Healing Journey

"Understand yourself; know yourself. Think about what makes you tick, about what could bring you out of bed in the morning, anxious to get started! Where is the joy in your life? What do you really want to do with your life? What is the thing that, if you could do it, would . . . bring a smile to your face, lift your heart in anticipation of each new day? When you follow your heart, it is amazing how quickly the universe responds with love."

— Pg. 41 Illusion's End:
Book Two A Pathway Toward Peace

L ike any adventure one embarks upon, you just have to start somewhere. My journey has led me to heal my mind, body and spirit and reclaim my life. It has now led me to share with you the revelation that if I was able to heal my mangled life and body, you can too. As with all things in this life, I am only addressing healing the body from *dis-ease* by stress or trauma. I am not addressing the spiritual or karmic reasons for *dis-ease*. One of the women who worked with me as I was healing was a therapist named Mary. She wasn't your ordinary run of the mill therapist and she nicknamed me "miracle child". I was given this nickname because she said she couldn't believe I had been through all that insanity and had anything viable left to work with. She also said, "It would be a real shame to have made it this far (to be alive and seeking help) and not make it all the way out."

Mary believed in me, and I can tell you that is the first step of your journey. You must find someone who believes in your ability to heal. She was one of my guides out of darkness and suffering. She could not heal me, just as I cannot heal you. I can share my experience with you, or at least part of my experience, and introduce you to the fact that you have your own inner navigational system. I needed to change my whole life and the way I approached how I lived my life for me to heal.

One of the first things I began to do was read. To inform myself about other options available to me besides the medical route. Our allopathic system of medicine can only take a person so far when suffering with stress related *diseases*. And, for the most part has not advanced to the point where they embrace the concept of healing from the inside out to help people fully heal. Our western system of medicine helps you live with pain and cope with whatever mental illness or *dis-ease* you have created. The system is not yet educating physicians on how to work with the whole person and to help them realize and understand that they themselves have responsibility in creating the pain and suffering in their bodies.

Allopathic medicine generally does not go looking for emotional, psychological and spiritual root causes, the energy behind the *dis-ease* or pain. They provide medicine for the symptoms, and if they can help reduce or alleviate your pain it is believed they've done their job. And many people don't know that there is anything different. As a matter of fact, the medical system is so overworked that it may even cause more damage than actual help, as I am sure many of you reading this may have experienced either yourself or with a family member. This system wanted me to be happy because I survived all the abuse and accepted that the painful existence I was experiencing was the best I could expect given the level of abuse I endured. My goal was not surviving anymore; my goal was to heal my life so that I could thrive.

I now read all kinds of different perspectives on healing with food, proper amounts of water, breathing, letting go of what thoughts I choose and learning how to live in the moment. After witnessing Troy's healing, I was excited and curious. Troy was able to heal at the rate he did because he was three years old with no built in resistance. I on the other hand was in my mid-twenty's when I began healing, which is important. Because the older you are before you begin to listen to your body and emotions, the more baggage and resistance you will have created, and this will have an impact on your healing journey.

When I began my journey, I was seriously resistant to change and new ideas. At the time, the thought of not going to the doctor every time my children or I didn't feel well seemed neglectful. I also believed that there had to be a drug or surgery that would "fix" my pain and *dis-eases* and that taking the time and effort to heal myself by getting to know myself was absurd. I also did not know that when we take medicine and prescription pills, we alter our body's natural chemistry and block the underlying problems from communicating with us. When people have surgery they alter their bodies, and it may or may not relieve the pain. However, if the surgery relieves the pain and a person doesn't uncover the underlying root cause for the pain it usually turns up somewhere else in your body.

You can learn to use the pain in your body to communicate with you and to help guide you back into your body and out of pain. If you disguise or cover up your pain and/or remove body parts, you cannot understand and feel how you're out of alignment with your higher self; which is the real source of most people's pain. I understand there are procedures and surgeries that are beneficial and that can help, and they are not going to interfere with the type of healing I'm discussing. It's not an all or nothing approach, it is an integrative approach that uses both systems to address the needs of the whole person.

On the other hand, the amount of gallbladder surgery women have because the root cause has not been addressed is disturbing. The energetic cause underneath the physical pain of an irritated gallbladder is "feeling of bitterness, feelings of anger, wanting to force things." (Karol, Pg. 246). Before having surgery, I would work with a student to help them uncover these unconscious feelings, unblock the energy and, if the person is truly committed to their healing and getting to the root cause, many times they can clear the negative energy out of their body. Then they will not require surgery. It takes time and requires honesty and commitment to loving thy self.

To aid in my healing, I have benefited from the many body workers who move energy out of the body or move energy in a way that releases old patterns of thoughts, feelings of anger, resentment, guilt, shame, and bitterness. Whether you are aware of these energies or not, if not released they can be held in and affect the body for your entire life. Body workers help to release these energies and blockages so that they can be replaced with love of self. I have used yoga, massage, acupuncture, Rolfing, deep cellular energy release, Reiki and a Shaman. I have used a few good therapists who are open-minded and believe in this type of work, because sometimes when you are healing you need to talk with someone who can help guide you through your emotions and feelings.

There will be times when you find yourself in one emotional chaotic situation after another, where everything seems at the point of breakdown, as you learn to listen to your body and not to other people. I have learned that a breakdown can lead to a break-through. Many times you will encounter family and friends who will want to derail your progress because your journey is having an adverse impact on their lives or they're just plain uncomfortable with the way you are now expressing yourself. Your ability to avoid reacting aggressively, becoming defensive and attempting to fight the difficulties head on will give you more energy to heal your life.

The journey towards self-healing requires that you are willing to enter the darkness of uncertainty within yourself. Becoming more aware of how you feel and what truly brings you into alignment with yourself and your highest good has its own timing and cannot be rushed. Information is revealed in its own time. Impatiently pushing for answers or seeking to hurry things along in the need to heal and get out of pain only prolongs the journey. I am now able to allow my life to unfold more easily and freely, listening to my body and my feelings and allowing them to take me on a journey every moment of the way to happiness and joy. I can only hope that in my sharing what I have experienced and learned, you may begin your journey to understanding yourself and living the life you want with happiness and joy.

Bibliography

Chopra, Deepak. *Creating Health: How to Wake Up the Body's Intelligence*. Massachusetts: Vantage Press. 1985.

Hay, Louise. L. *Heal You Body*. California: Hay House. 1982.

Hay, Louise. L. *You Can Heal Your Life*. California: Hay House. 1984.

Morris, Francis M. *Illusion's End: Book Two A Pathway toward Peace*. Arizona: OPA Publishing. 2006.

Marooney, Kimberly. *Angel Blessings*. California: Merrill-West Publishing. 1995.

Pearsall, Paul. *The Heart's Code: Tapping the Wisdom and Power of Our Heart Energy*. New York: Bantam Doubleday Dell Publishing. 1998.

Myss, Caroline. *Why People Don't Heal and How They Can.* New York: Harmony Books. 1997.

Myss, Caroline. *Invisible Acts of Power: Personal Choices That Create Miracles*. New York: Free Press. 2004.

Quotes Pictures.net. Posted on 17/09/2012 by Quotes Pics in 1280x800, Mad Hatter, Quotes Pictures *http://quotes pictures.net/quote-pictures/have-i-gone-mad-quote-from-alice-in-wonderland/*, March 14, 2014.

Retherford, Ralph. E. *When Chicken Soup is Not Enough: Revolutionary Healing through the Mind-Body Connection*. Florida: Frederick Fell Publishers, Inc. 1999.

Tolle, Eckhart. *The Power of Now*. Canada: Namaste Publishing. 1997.

Truman, Karol. K. *Feelings Buried Alive Never Die . . .* Utah: Olympus Distributing. 2003.

About the Author

Donna Marie Vigilante has been a yoga practitioner since 1994. She completed her 200 hours (RYT) of yoga Anusara Teacher Training Program with Betsey Downing at Garden of the Heart Yoga Center in Sarasota Florida in 2005. Donna Marie is a certified 1st and 2nd degree Reiki healer. She also owns and operates Mountain Yoga and Healing in Maryville, Tennessee. She has taught for Penland School of Crafts in North Carolina and has recently accepted a position teaching yoga at the University of Tennessee Non-credit courses. Donna Marie holds a Masters in Psychology from the University of North Florida and a Juris Doctorate from Stetson University College of Law. She raised two sons (James and Troy) and has two grandchildren (Kellin and Cecilia).